DEDICATION

To all the souls who have contributed
to my life journey
and
inspired the words within these pages.
Thank you.

CONTENTS ...

THE CONTENTS IN THIS BOOK
ARE THE REAL DEAL FOR
ALL THE
COOL KATS ....

ACKNOWLEDGMENTS

Thank you to Alfonso Siverls for your wisdom and humor.

Thank you to my loyal and loving friends.

Thank you to my Mom and Family for all their unconditional love and wisdom.

I love you Tony y Tete!

My Smokey Bronx Blues
September 6, 2013

Arising from the well Of

Deep burgundy hues

Float the remnants Of

My Smokey Bronx Blues

traveling over white stones

And along City streets

where cultures mingle

To a unified beat.

Underneath dull concrete skin

Are pulsating electric veins

That host silver bullets decorated

In graffiti blood stains.

Holy brown highrises are blessed

By Saint Mary in the park

Where Cypress trees linger

By Brooks after dark.

My eyes have gazed upon

Splendid and Sound Views

In the journey I Call

My Smokey Bronx Blues.

Joy of Sight
February 20, 2013

To observe the undying culture
in motion and gaze upon
the beauty of those
who sustain it
is one of the most
precious of our
Creator's gifts.

Millin
October 23, 2013

Yellow and white,
Yellow and white
Yellow and white.
Sunlight and rays of light
Are the joy that Millin
Brings when she dances,
Dances on pretty brown
Toes
Glazed and seasoned
By barrels with voices
Oh, the joyous
Overflow of rhythm
When Millin dances.

To Norka's Mom,

With deep appreciation for placing seeds in the Bronx.

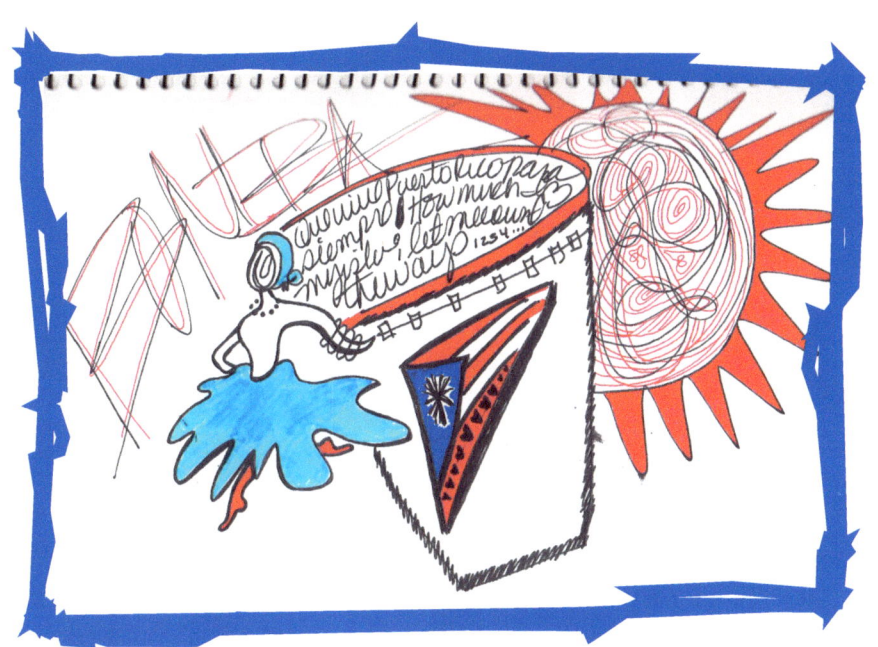

The Bomballectual
May 24, 2013

The Real Bronx

Is the home of

The Bomballectual,

A socially conscious,

intellectual,

Bomba Practitioner

Whose scarlet liquid

Identity is concealed

In the heart.

Dear Friend,
February 20, 2013

You said "I'm gettin' old"
to which I reply:
"You are in transition
much like a caterpillar
returning to your
youth in intervals
related to the seasons
of the Earth, I foresee
meeting you again in warmer
climate and exchanging,
as we do now,
the intellectual and spiritual
wisdom that has been
invaluable
and as meaningful
to me as the wind
that touches my skin
and maintains my life."

To Alfonso,

Your friendship and guidance is a treasure that will remain within my heart for always, thank you!

Writers write to right the wrongs, or so I've been told.

Classified, Filed and Stored
Began in 2003
Completed on April 4, 2013 at a bookstore in Co-Op City, Bronx

I have been classified, filed
and stored
First name: JASMIN
Last name: RIVERA
I am a Pisces
Born on March 20th of the year
1975
I am the personality
You read about in the morning
horoscope page
My skin is Brown and my
genes are a size 32
Puerto Rican
This is who you say
I am
But I have classified my Self
alongside the Sons of Mayaguez*,
Filed my consciousness at the base
of the Jibaro's mountains
And Stored my Heart
where You can never find it.

I Like to Count
February 11, 2013

One, three, 2013
I'm counting
On you to ease
the mathematical
lessons that
left in me a trench,
gradually flooding
with wisdom,
as the reality of
the subtraction of
Loved Ones
sinks in.

The B-Boyz Generation
2013
Wrote during a Bronx arts organization writer's workshop.

We skipped the letter "A"
And moved into the
B-Boy Generation
When so many
B-Boyz wanted to
B-come men
Who were respected
Their mouths made
rhythms that were
Unexpected
Their Addidas clothed
bodies moved with
electrified ancestor memories
A uniform cluster
of Bs
"Hey B,
What it B-like?"
"Yo B that's
so Fresh B!"
We skipped E
and left it for
the next generation
and got
Struck at C
R ... A
C and K
"Hey B, can

you spare some change
cuz' I can't afford to recite
a reversed alphabet"
Backs turned,
As B
faded away to
Hip-Hop Heaven

To Jito,

Thank you, my sweet brother, for your last words of wisdom.

Utopia
2013

As I walk around

Metropolis

It becomes clear to me

that Fresco's Round City

Remains a square in your imagination

rather than free circles within circles

that illuminate the spirit-mind

Oh, what a nightmare

the imprisonment and prostitution

of Mathematics

To coexist

To coexist

Oh what a joy

it would be

To coexist.

My Makeba Medicine

I've found my eternal
medication,
3 tongue-clicks cures
the societal
mind-sedation
A disease that
attempts to seize
My Light
My Makeba inoculates
Me from the sleaze
in this Life.

August 7, 2013

Project Blues

Blue sat by my
Bed last night,
Night lights eavesdropping
on the stream of words
I confessed
We talked through the
Sounds of the City sirens,
With every car that
drove by a spotlight
Caste my words
Into moving shadows
that danced on my
ceiling and
I remembered
When she read
poems to me as
a Child,
Sliced my naive
breast and replaced
it with armor.
And you Blue,
You
Always remind
me of such things.

To Dee, One of my first teachers in life, thank you sis, I love you.

When one encompasses compassion as vast as the depths of the ocean it is imperative to move slow so that all can feed from the fish in your sea.

February 20, 2013

Frivolous Masculinity
2013

Title created on October 07, 2011
Transformed on March 30, 2013

Modern masculinity has masked
the nature of a Man.
Like Great Lions dressed
in Candy-Striped Carnival Dresses
They now wears pants that
fall below their asses
Not knowing that
they are now assets
to the Great Consumer
of Culture and Identity.

A Poem to You
2012

A poem to you
the one who
created a collage
from the best
parts of friends
and lovers,
that you now hang
from a silver necklace,
A slow moving facade
encased in a shell
designed not to reveal
the rejection-fearing Self
Warming it's frame
with pieces of borrowed
intellectual
and inspirational flesh
from those you surround
A cloak worn
especially to impress
and hide
your vulnerability.

Inheritance
2012

There exists wisdom
in the corners of the ghetto
which is my concrete
intellectual meadow
Where the progeny of flowers

replant and sow
replant and sow
replant and sow

the genetically inherited
memory of Our ancestors

DNA
DNA
DNA

That Does-not-Die
Even when exposed
to dilutions of
poisoned illusions

How I survive
How I survive
How I survive

On silver speeding trains
of tragedy
just to ride the waves of
color-by-number bliss
but I don't forget to plant
and sow
DNA
So that I can survive
from generation to generation

to generation
to generation
to generation

During these periods of
extreme expression
in nature
We are reminded
that we are delicate
visitors
upon this Earth
and that we should
be humble in our
innovations.

March 11, 2011

Ode to Muse
April 24, 2012

In conversations you paint
Words with Ghetto spray cans,
Intoxicating the lungs –
Lungs that give birth
to rhythm and movement –
Movements which I
Have no dominion over
Because it is you, oh
Soulful Muse who quickens
The pace of my pulse,
Lifts the darkened veil
From blind hearts,
Until truth yells at
The light.
Enlightened by your
Beauty I fingerprint
Expressions of eternal
Love in countless
Hues of blood
Until like lovers
On a midnight
Beach I die
Over and over
again.

On the Topic of Crack Cocaine
October 12, 2012

Contemplating my brother's
slow death
I imagine the
ingredients that
combined and conspired
to bring him here.
I can forgive
But I can't forget
the murderers
of my paternal links.

Population Study
March 6, 2008

Statistics/Methods course @ C. University, Math building.

I lie to you everyday
No matter how much
You perfect your survey
Figure me out
you never will
I evolve by the
minutes you instill

Rhegos of Regolith
May 9, 2011

She hides
Her emotions under
Rhegos of regolith,
Powdery and
Dull with age.

Her piscatorial
adventures
taking her in Circles

Across globes
Hip-hoping on
Honey-Brown
Heels into
the Bronx
to the Caribbean
and back.

Feminine Power
December 7, 2011

Feminine Power is
mistaken for sexuality
mistaken for Bitchy-ness
mistaken for submission
Just listen
as I
clarify
the
misunderstanding.
By the divine right of Mother Nature
I am within my right to express sexuality
without being labeled a whore.
By the divine right of Mother Nature
I lead my children with a firm hand
because the world is a hard place.
By the divine right of Mother Nature
I bow my head when I know that it is necessitated.
By the divine right of Mother Nature
I was designed to move the World toward
the correct path,
and I will.
And I am –
despite
trite
reasonings
of man.

Distortion
October 7, 2011

On the #8 Bus passing through the Barrio on 3rd Avenue

How can we understand the world around us when cannibals distort the definitions of meaning?
Consider the word: Freedom

Is there not a
price to pay for
the oration of
the oppressed?

Is Democracy
equaled to it?

And what of
Equality?

Are we equal
only to Your
prior existence?

And will we
ever be equal
to You in the
present?

07312011

Oh, how Life does transform the mind –
but not the heart
The heart ...
where ego falsely resides, cemented to regret,
Regrets ....
something the air is denied sound from my lips,
My Lips ...
that once whispered a mute promise of shared love,
Whispering Love!
oh, how love transforms the mind –
but not the heart,
the heart –
the heart –
the heart –
still beating,
in its vain egotistical rhythm,
Will not permit me
to share with the air the longing for Love.

Walking through Harlem
2010

I have walked

the Harlem steps

of Brother X

From my journey

as a Science Gypsy

to Poughkeepsie

on the 125th St. train,

to the red-bricked

Itchy-Ivy atmosphere,

where blood smeared

in order for me to

concentrate on

the Study of my Selves.

What is the Price of a Child?
2010

Written during one of my graduate courses on human rights with Professor Becker. Comment on U.S. policy regarding child soldiers in Africa.

The seeds of sacrifice
lay the foundation
for funeral beds
sprinkled with Baby Breaths,
Negotiations stain the
fixed image of compassion
stirring Humans to Watch
for the Right turn in
the Wrong direction

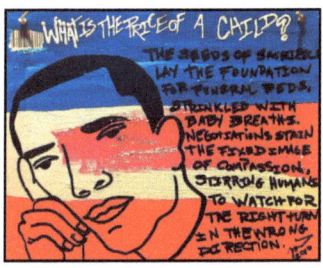

Image: The Almonte Collection, Double-Sided Acrylic on Canvas
Santiago, Dominican Republic.

The Mickey Dee's Embassy
June 5, 2010
ICE Train from Bochum to Amsterdam

Feel safe –
Oh weary Northern traveler
For at every foreign stop
is an embassy,
recognized by all and
universally neutral.
Where you can be guaranteed
that at least one
person speaks English.
When culture is
unfamiliar,
feet are soar,
your lost with no map ...
do not panic –
For the Golden Fries
of Freedom
will ease your
burgarless burdens.
So, curious Northern wanderer
relieve your anxieties
and take flight
into the welcoming
world that is yours.

Hill Street Blues in Amsterdam
2010

Light up a piece of cheese

Y desfruta the ambiance

At the blues

smoke cafe

In Amsterdam

My heart is missing you

And singing with Lena Horn

"Ohhh how I adore you,

Ohhh how I miss you!"

Read the sign - it's a warning:

Don't let the city

pick-pocket your

heart!

We will return together

And smile with these blues

At Hill Street Blues

in Amsterdam.

Red Light, Red Light, Red Light, Red Light, You don't have to put on the …

"… i'll aLwaYs lOve yOu.."
 —CHanGe tHe cHaNneL jAzZ !

... tHe wHeEls oN tHe bUs gO rOuND and rOuND ....

I Sense the Hunger
July 27, 2010

I sense the hunger
from the back of my
cool ankle,
As pollen dreams
enter my mind
The Aging Womb
desires
The Suns Attention
And time
is my enemy.

On My Way Home

I am so excited to be returning
Home
Home being your warm embrace,
Your sweet scent,
Beautiful voice,
Tender whispers.
Home is where the heart is,
My heart is with you forever, forever, forever....

Wall
October 6, 2010

The wall is indeed charming as I peak at it from afar at the bar across the street. Who likes it? Why ask? I don't care who doesn't .. Really I don't. It's the beauty of age! Take it or leave it. Either way - I was able to share it the way I wanted to. This is an Ode to MY GAY ART! 2010

Image: The Almonte Collection, Santiago, Dominican Republic.

Mi Hermano

JEAN-MICHEL WAS MY BROTHER,
FROM ANOTHER BORIQUA MOTHER.
DON'T LET PUERTO RICAN SHADES
CONFUSE AND DAZE -
YOUR INHERENT SENSES.
I KNOW THAT SOMETIMES
EL PEIL IS A DISTRACTION -
BLINDING YOUR EYES
FROM TALENT AND ACTION.
WHEN ALL THAT MATTERED
TO MY BROTHER
WAS NOT THAT THE POCKET
GOT FATTER -
BUT RATHER
THAT YOU FREED YOUR MIND.

JASMIN RIVERA NOVEMBER 28, 2010

Everyone Wants to be Oppressed:
In dedication to the privileged
May 21, 2009

Everyone wants to be oppressed
Popping pills to relieve
fictitious stress
Vassar Blond Babies
tear when they are excluded
from propaganda designed
to keep the mind diluted

Island Walk
2009

On my way to class and as I waited for the light to change colors in the heart of Hunts Point in the Bronx a beautiful Cuban woman crosses the street. How do I know that this woman is Cuban you ask. She lives around my neighborhood and I have seen her before and heard her speak, oh yeah she is Cuban, not because I say so but because she said so!

La Negra Cubana
she still has that
island walk,
Belly out
Red-blue hair
Ba-Boom, Ba-Boom
from left to right
right to left
When she walk

La Negra Cubana
she still has that
island walk,
head high up
in the air
arms swing, swing, swing
back and forth
forth and back
When she walk

Still-free-spirit
island walk
no socks
in her sneakers
neon-green-glitter
spandex
Ya!

La Negra Cubana
she still has that
island walk.

Joe Cuba's Funeral

2009

I was working at !AHA! when Joe Cuba transcended to the celestial tarisma

He was viewed by all
who loved him at the
Ortiz Funeral Home on
204 East 116th St.
Between Avenues 2 and 3
On the 18th and 19th days
from 2 to 10PM

He will been missed
but not forgotten

Image: The Kathleen Benson Collection, *East Harlem Under Construction*
New York City, El Barrio, United States

What do I say on this form?

Ethnicity

☐ Puerto Rican

Race

☐ European
settled in the New World,
their biological stowaways
committed genocide on a noble nation,
which was then replaced by the
inheritors of the Earth, mix – shake well
and pour ....

> I can identify with my maternal
> Spanish grandfather because I'm
> light-skinned enough
> but my blood
> is not red
> My skin is not White
>
> I check the only box
> that makes me "feel"
> comfortable ...

☐ Black or African-American

Who can hang with Revolutionaries?
2009

Written in the back of a flyer from a bronx woman's organization announcing an event honoring womyn of Puerto Rican descent who were/and are a part of the Puerto Rican Independence movement

Who can hang with Revolutionaries?
Certainly not me
with all their music and colored beads,
fearless walk through unmarked streets,
People who stand their ground
but fly with their feet

Who can hang with Revolutionaries?
I don't think I can
'cause what I cover with
a thumbnail
they cover with their hand

Who can hang with Revolutionaries?
She said I could,
since I'm a poetry
packing mama
from the hood

Who can hang with Revolutionaries?
I think I will –
just to watch
children play,
while time
stands still.

My Nose, My Nose
2008

Caribbean History course with Dr. Carlos Sanabria, PhD.

My nose,
my nose
can sometimes
fool those who would
like to see me lighter
and spiritually exposed
When I was a child with small
hands I choose to examine this nose
whose point I felt was mutiltated like my
toes

I used
to look at Mami's
nose and wonder if
mine would look like her pointy, straight nose
My nostrils were wider and browner back then
but later shrank and became lighter
It ceased to look like
Papi's nose and
my hope that
it would be
a replica
of his-
Wide,
Brown
and
flaring
when
he
smiled
faded -
like
my skin.

The Mental Block
August 4, 2008

Schermerhorn, @ C. University, 8th floor

Artificial light makes
a lot of noise
but for now I use it
'cause my Sun has been
stolen by the bourgeois
I read false language
on a White sheet
with Black letters
that run with fast feet
the only words
that stick in my head
are always the
one's left unsaid
"So why bother reading?"
you asked me last night
"Cause my head was left
bleeding with my bandage
not tight
and a Helmet on my brain
to block out the light
figured that the Black evening
would allow my mind to take
flight
but I was stranded
again under
this Artificial light.

Self Discovery
September 25, 2007

Being that each man
carries the life of
God in his soul
It would make
sense that in order
to reach God
Man must first
seek himself
and reach out
Once this act
is accomplished
each man will
see himself for
the first time
And since it
is said that,
"Man was made
in the image
of God"
The peace & unity
that will result
will allow
Man to fulfill
His ultimate Destiny
"Becoming God".

A Letter to the Astronomic Pioneer
2007

You think you know something
about the stars
Looking devices pulled from
Cracker Jack Boxes
Selling false knowledge
Like Foxes
Who daily, pose as self-proclaimed profits
You know only that you want to
know something of which
you know nothing about

Legacies
Began in February 20, 2007
Title created April 11, 2013

The seeds of my mother, now weeds on your land
Cease to grow, overwhelm my sickled hand
Pain is accepted, its love you can't stand
Winds so tired of blowing they drop ears in the sand
All red
enough said
Leave no scripture for the next generation.

Conversations with Mami

Yellow Bright Rose
July 2004

Riding on the Bx19

toward Southern Boulevard

I gazed upon a sight

which left me awed

A yellow bright rose,

growing among blades

of concrete grass

I'd like to suppose

that the Creator

blossomed it for me

But I know it is

there for more than

just my eyes to see.

WISDOM

Ohh,
the pain
of acquiring
wisdom,
how it aches
the Aging Spirit.

May 22, 2013

Treasures Are
June 13 2013

Family photos
that you have
not seen since
you were a child.

Just New York
July 24, 2013

Just New York
Is how her
poem starts,
With the pen
In her hand
and the moon
In her heart.
Just New York
and no other land
Will permit time
To wash from
her eyes each
granule Of sand
Just New York
Can give you the
Beauty to which
Your prose aspires
With mega-high rises
And slow-syrup desires
It's just New York
That calls to your soul
Come back, come
Back
To the place you
Know.

To Arlene,
The global trekker whose a New Yorker at heart.

Its Just Life: Chapter 1
August 16, 2013

We complain about our "misfortune"

Forgetting about the decisions

We made that brought us

To that point in our lives,

If we take the time to see

so-called "misfortunes" as

Opportunities provided to

Us by our Creator we would

Discover how quickly

"Misfortune" transforms into

Success through a deeper

Understanding of ourselves.

In Conversations

October 5, 2013

In a Sugar and Bean conversation
with my ancestors
I was reminded to always finish
that which I have begun
So that I would always
discover the answers
to all my inquiries.

photo: copyright Jasmin Rivera 2013

Para mi Riveras
November 2, 2013

Mirror, mirror on the wall
Why can't Rivera eyebrows
Be small,
And why are some of them so tall?
And why do they talk so loud, laugh so hearty and walk
so proud?!
And where can I find one
whose not as stubborn
as a mule?
And one who doesn't
Drink Bustelo to refuel?
Oh mirror, mirror on the wall
Will the Riveras always be
The finest of them all?

Year of the Hoochie Mamas

November 20, 2013 10:14 PM

2014 is the year of the
Hoochie Mamas
Nails and hair of all colors,
Sparkle spandex
Glitter Glamours Strut on
Hard concrete,
She-
Makes everything Beautiful.
The Holy Virgin
of St. Mary's Park
Misunderstood
In lewd dreams
After dark
When she unveils
tall tales
are told,
When she exhales
all man's
faults unfold.

BORICUA WISDOM # 1
DECEMBER 2, 2013

WHEN WE ARE INJURED
OUR BODIES CREATE
A DEFENSE TO PROTECT
FROM INFECTION
AND FURTHER INJURY
BUT THESE SCABS
ARE NOT ATTRACTIVE
THEY ARE HARD AND CRUSTY
BUT THEY PROTECT OUR
OPEN WOUNDS.
DON'T TRY TO PEEL
PEOPLE'S SCABS -
THEY ARE THERE FOR
A REASON.
LET THEM BE,
WHEN THEY HEAL
THE SCAB WILL
FALL OFF ON ITS OWN.

How Do You Create?
December 3, 2013

Creation is not random
there is a purpose
and meaning in it.

Some get side tracked,
swept up in the idea
of their creativity.

Drummers are drummers
but not all drummers
are alike
What kind of drummer are you?

Painters are painters
but not all painters
see the same colors
or know how to speak
with them
Do you know how to use
your colors?

And finally,
and this is my
favorite ...

Singers are singers
but – well
not all singers can bring down
the Sun from the sky,
or guide the wind under
your green palm skirt

So I ask you,
What kind of singer are you?

My talent
is that everything
to me is art.

My fault
is that everything
to me is art.

Poems of the Broken Heart # 1
December 12 2013

The duct of my eye
Is filled with puddles
Of heartache
A wound so deep
That a band aid
The size of the
Infinite universe
Can not cover.

                                                    1:11
  A time to realize that the number One haunts us
                                                              all.

Pull and push the word
Called Love
Tug and tear
The sentiments
It stands for
But don't ever
Believe that it
Will withstand
Such harsh treatment.

Right now
I overstand the
Unrealized thirst
One is left with
From the lack
Of appreciation
By others.

The Great Artist

The process of becoming
A Great Artist is painful.
How does one convey poetry
Of the dying heart
If one has never perished from
Love taken away?
The Great Artist paints the
Woman so beautifully
Because it was the last
Time he would capture
Her adoration of him.
How does one pluck the Blues
If one has never been used,
And then discarded?
The Greatest of Artists
Bleed to death slowly
While all the world looks
Upon their masterpieces.

I have
received
ruff
rugged
returns
For half a life
Dedicated
to your
safely
supplied
sustenance.

December 12, 2013

*

Forced to experience the darkness ....
                I found the path to my Light.

Poems of the Broken Heart # 2
December 13, 2013

The Thin Line

Really?! It's 4:00 am ...
We'll, it's really 4:09 AM,
To be exact
And we all know how
Much I appreciate
The safety of precision
In fact,
It's what made you
Love me and then
Hate me –
Exactly in that order.

Salty Sorrows

Broken chest plates
Cover the battlefield,
The stench of
Gun powder and flesh
Mix together in my
Narrow nasal passages
The air is filled with
salty sorrows of yesterday
And we can't take back
The shots that were fired
that ended our world.

Rants of An Insomniac

December 14, 2013

Who else is up contemplating
Their journey in this life?
Considering all that has come full circle?
In wonder of how the Creator designed your life's lessons?
Confused, wise, grateful and stubborn to move forward all at once?
Maybe it's just me.

Insomnia – 4:55AM

The love that drips
Through Paralyzed
Finger slits
Slips away,
Slowly
And there
Is nothing
You can do
To stop it.

Insomnia – 5:22AM

I'm laying here staring
at an old black and white
photo of my mother's
mother–
A Puerto Rican Mulatta
who met an early death,
taken from her seven small children because the family could
not afford the tuberculosis treatment that could have saved
her.
I see
my uncle and aunt in this picture and my mother in Abuela's
womb,
all oblivious to the path that has been set for them;
a path of bleeding thorns that would lead me to
my well of endless faith
and perseverance.
No matter what
Boogie crashing,
Bronx bashing
Frustrations color my life
In hot shots of red lightening
I find my way up because
my maternal inheritance is
the map of the crescent moon. My mother had to stand
even when she fell,
she learned to do this
because she had to survive – Mami taught me to survive.
Thank you Mami.
I love you.

When Brooklyn speaks To Bronx volumes of wisdom are recorded.

Urban Meditation and Relaxation

December 14, 2013

I sneak out of reality
from time to time
And head to
Painter's Paradise
Where trees are rolled
And smoked
Over a constant Fogon
I go there a minute
Before I'm too far gone
I enter through the
Rabbit's Door
Hopping over
Psychedelic Daisies
In hopes that maybe
I'll discover
the Answer
In bright **Lime**, **teal** and
Mandarin colors.

Poetry
December 14, 2013

Oh Poetry,
What a friend you
Are to me!
You listen
Without judgement
and provide a blank
Slate for me to
Chronicle the
Sentiment of my soul's
Experiences.

Aggo
December 15, 2013

I fall asleep to the
Lullabies of my ancestors
The past and future
Rock me back and forth
To rest from the present
Day
Turning into night
I'm always turning
Toward the night
With keys in hand
As I respond to
The crossroad
Of my dreams,
Aggo Eleggua!

The Nuyorican Senses
December 15, 2013

What does it smell like to
Be a Nuyorican?
The invasion of the aroma
Of Mami's gandules
On a winter day in the Bronx.
What does it sound like to
be Nuyorican?
The voice of Tato Torres in the sala,
the loud conversation over the music
so you don't have to lower the volume.
What does it feel like to
be Nuyorican?
Hugs from Mami, smiles of pride from Papi
and long conversations with your brothers
and sisters.
What does it taste like to
be Nuyorican?
Salty, sweet, hard, soft, bitter,
But always...
Always...
Delicious.

Poems of the Broken Heart # 3
December 15, 2013

NO CUSSING ALLOWED

BECAUSE YOU SAID TO KEEP IT CLEAN AND NOT CUSS:

JOAISDNENFJNCIUSDCNDJBSB DJS
DJHBFJEFKJBFKJBDSFASDNLKDNKL
KBJKJNKJBKJBJBKAJBFKFJBKJBKJBFKJB
FKJF
JOAISDNENFJNCIUSDCNDJBSB DJS
DJHBFJEFKJBFKJBDSFASDNLKDNKL
KBJKJNKJBKJBJBKAJBFKFJBKJBKJBFKJB
FKJF
JOAISDNENFJNCIUSDCNDJBSB DJS
DJHBFJEFKJBFKJBDSFASDNLKDNKL
KBJKJNKJBKJBJBKAJBFKFJBKJBKJBFKJB
FKJF

AND THAT'S ALL!

PLUM, PLUM WINE

SLOWLY SLIPPING INTO

INTOXICATION

ON WINE MADE OF PLUM

IRON THOUGHTS PRESS MY MIND

AND I BECOME NUMB.

I WONDER WHO I HAVE BEEN AND

NOW WHO I WILL BECOME.

I WAIT FOR RELIEF FROM

HOT BROWN LIQUID

THAT NEVER ARRIVES

BUT LORD KNOWS HOW I TRY

TO SMILE LIKE THE

GOOD-GIRL CLOWN

WHILE I QUIETLY AND PAINFULLY

DRINK THIS SORROW DOWN.

Surviving

December 16, 2013

Roar ....
Like a lion awaiting it's destiny
Swim ...
like the fish preparing to mate
Fight ....
like a woman trying to keep sanity.

BORICUA WISDOM # 2
DECEMBER 16, 2013

WALKING AND RUNNING

ARE TWO DIFFERENT THINGS

YOU WALK TO ARRIVE AT YOUR

DESTINATION

WITH WISDOM AND SPIRITUAL

KNOWLEDGE

YOU RUN WHEN YOU CAN'T WAIT

TO GET THERE

AND REALIZE THAT YOU MISSED

THE MOST IMPORTANT THINGS

BECAUSE YOU WERE RUSHING.

Dedication to Social Media

Post Post Post Post Post Post Post Post Post Post Post Post Post
Post Post Post Post Post Post Post Post Post Post Post Post
Post Post Post Post Post Post Post Post Post Post Post Post
Post Post Post Post Post Post Post Post Post Post Post Post
Post Post Post Post Post Post Post Post Post Post Post Post
Post Post Post Post Post Post Post Post Post Post Post Post
Post Post Post Post Post Post Post Post Post Post Post Post
Post Post Post Post Post Post Post Post Post Post Post Post
Post Post Post Post Post Post Post Post Post Post Post Post
Post Post Post Post Post Post Post Post Post Post Post Post
Post Post Post Post Post Post Post Post Post Post Post Post
Post Post Post Post Post Post Post Post Post Post Post Post
Post Post Post Post Post Post Post Post Post Post Post Post
Post Post Post Post Post Post Post Post Post Post Post Post
Post Post Post Post Post Post and Post Post PostPost Post Post Post
Post Post Post Post Post Post Post
 Post Post Post Post Post Post Post Post Post Post Post Post
Post Post Post Post Post Post Post Post Post Post Post Post
Post Post Post Post Post Post Post Post Post Post Post Post
Post Post Post Post Post Post Post Post Post Post Post Post
Post Post Post Post Post Post Post Post Post Post Post Post
Post Post Post Post Post Post Post Post Post Post Post Post
Post Post Post Post Post Post Post Post Post Post Post Post
Post Post Post Post Post **Post Post Post Post Post Post Post**
Post Post Post Post Post Post Post Post Post Post Post Post
Post Post Post Post Post Post Post Post Post Post Post Post
Post Post Post Post Post Post Post Post Post Post Post Post
Post Post Post Post Post Post Post Post Post Post Post Post
Post Post Post Post Post Post Post Post Post Post
and Post Post Post Post Post Post Post Post Post some more!!!!!!!!

Please don't drop coins
in the water fountain,
It makes no sense
to try and pay
off the universe
to make your
dreams come true
with chump change.

December 16, 2013

The Daily Gossip
December 16, 2013

It has come to the attention of the
international community
that the heart and the mind are
no longer cooperating in the
peace talks that were set forth in previous years.

What everyone wants to know is
how the heart and mind will once again
resolve the crisis that has impacted the
rest of the physical and spiritual international community?

Correspondents for the
Heart Times and Mindful Memoirs
are in opposition as to the outcome of
how the mind will react to the break in
international relations.

Reporter Mrs. Logic Under Pressure argued that,
"The Mind has too often conceded to the requests of the Heart."

Stating that she believes that
the new talks will bring new policies forward while
Ms. XoXo Besos pointed out that, "the heart is a leader in the
international community and will undoubtably exert it's power
position to win domestic and foreign support."

The talks will continue as the international community awaits
either a change in policy or the same business as usual.

The Good Fish

December 16, 2013

One fish,
two fish
I'm trying real hard to
be a good fish
But I can only swim in
this direction
for a short time
until I switch
direction suddenly
and without warning
I am a Whale that has engulfed all
the life around me!

Latino Pop Art Postcard Series.
The Tirado Family Collection. 2012

Poems of the Broken Heart # 4
December 16, 2013

Fallen

Hopeless Romantics
fall helplessly into
despair when their feet
touch the earth

Nothin'

No sleep
No more Sweet Golden
Plum Wine
No more comfort
No Home
No number two
No addition
Only subtraction
Only hunger
Only thirst.

I

i remember when I
expressed colors
Flaring with maroon
and cobalt blue
i was not I,
she stood tall
and yelled loud
And now
i
is trying to find
her colors again.

Transformations

The branch
was thick with bark
and thorns,
Over the seasons
It became a flexible
twig with dark
brown dots
and leaves.
I never imagined
that
Tomorrow it
would become
a Tree
that bears fruit
and sprouts
Roots.

Ode to 12:30AM

You are the twelve o'clock hour of transformation
for all the 59 minutes that make you
who you are
I thank you
for today will be a new opportunity
to re-invent myself
despite the heartache
and frustrations.

1:11AM

Here you are again
loyal and dependable
the # to the ancestral road

On the Topic of Ancestors

Aguadilla, Puerto Rico
will never be absent
from my consciousness,
It is and has been
the leading factor of
my understanding of the world
and is now the fuel
that moves this Train!

Touch Down

My feet are touching
the mushy, fresh Earth
A feeling new to me
As I have been floating
Above the realm.

WELCOME!

DECEMBER 16, 2013

TONIGHT
THE COCOON
HAS CRACKED
AND WHAT BEGINS
TO FLUTTER
AT THE SURFACE
OF THE LEFT OVER
SHELL
IS THE REALIZATION
THAT OYA
HAS MADE HER
PRESENCE
KNOWN IN
MY LIFE.

ACHE.

The Process of Letting Go

December 16, 2013

Breath,
Breath,
and then exhale.
It will happen
regardless of
whether you
want it to
or not.
Let go,
Let go,
because you
can not
hold tight
to a free bird.
Just wait,
Just wait,
the wind
may return
washed away
treasure.

Wonderful Wilfredo!

December 17, 2013

Student Inspiration at Hostos in the BX

When you hesitate to dream
Wonderful Wilfredo appears
reminding you to
let go of fears
and replace them with
hope and motivation.
Thank you
Wonderful Wilfredo!

Poems of a Heart In Transition #1

Delta Aquilea

January 4, 2014 6:18am

I beg on bended knee
that the Left arm
of Delta Aquilea
no more sets
it's site on me
For I have been
consumed by
Fire's Pain of
parting
And no longer
Know who
I am.

The Body is the Home
January 4, 2014 9:18am

The body is the home
My Body is my own
Your sudden vacancy
was paired with
the eviction of
my dreams
Your Body was my home
but now I am alone,
no furniture –
My spirit stirs
in constant motion
with unsaid things
and emotions.

Rage
January 4, 2014 9:20am

Rage
feelings in a cage
never knew
this hurt
but
like a brief
and sudden wind
under a skirt
it snuck
upon me and tore
me to pieces.

More of You, Less of Me

January 4, 2014 9:45am

More Lipstick,
more pain
More nails,
more hurt
More shakes,
more cracks
More fashion,
more heartache
More of you,
Less of me ....

Parking Lot Therapy
January 4, 2014 9:48am

Cigarette swearing,
Blind driving
through
storms of icicles
piercing my heart,
piercing my heart,
and piercing my heart
over and over again

Your Mine
January 4, 2014 10:03am

I'm slipping away
further
and further
from who I
once was
when You said,
"Your Mine."
Don't kill me!
Don't kill me!!
Don't kill me!!!
Breath life back
into this dying
heart.

I was a Lighthouse

January 4, 2014 10:15am

I was
a Lighthouse
through the
storm
Made of brick
and mortar
Your ship's
constant
destination
but now your
journey
has wondered
into the unknown
and My Light
you vanquished.

Back Alley Bulldog
January 4, 2014 10:19am

The back alley bulldog
Is a creature that is
chained at the gates
of gas stations,
fed but unloved,
unwanted and
unnoticed.
The Bitches
bark and sniff
every time
lovers pass by
hand in hand ...
Mouth salivating
with envy,
Belly ravenous to
sink rabid teeth
into Beautiful flesh.
Your unchecked
Insecurities now
leave you vulnerable
to stray Bitches.

I'm There
January 4, 2014 10:23am

I'm there
I know that now.
No matter how you
run
You will not
escape it
because I'm still
there
Empty sala
Empty kitchen
filled with me
Shower streams
of memory
haunt you now,
will haunt you later,
and forever
and yet
you still
run
run
run
run
to Empty arms.

Next Stop?

January 4, 2014 10:23am

I don't know where

the next turn is

my compass fogged

what was horizontal

is now vertical

training myself for

Cervical Amnesia

forget,

forget,

forget,

how you felt inside me.

Darkness
January 6, 2014 10:05am

The darkness is overwhelming
Engulfed in shades of navy blue black
I hear the ghosts of the past creeping
up on me from behind as I run, run, run
toward the light that seems so far away.

My Life
January 6, 2014 10:03am

My life has
changed suddenly
What once was love
accepted abundantly
is now taken from another
You want her as your
New Lover
but what of friendship
I know you ran away
but didn't know
you would slip
I want to reach
out to you
as I once did
but I know it
will cut my head off
in the process.

Forgive Yourself

Forgive yourself for being
naive and in love
For blinding your sight
to what you always knew
was wrong and right
For the times you ignored
your instincts not to satiate
your addictive devotion
Forgive yourself
for blaming yourself
for the pain someone
else has caused you!

January 6, 2014 10:14am

STOP CALLING ON ME!

January 6, 2014 10:07am

Stop calling on me

for moments of

consolation,

Your pride &

arrogance

are

notorious &

brazen.

Your masked

selfishness

was never

apparent to

Me –

today I

Know better.

FRANKENSTEIN'S REMEDY FOR A BROKEN HEART

JANUARY 6, 2014 10:11AM

CUT THE SHOULDER
THAT COMFORTS
THE ONE WHO
HURT YOU,

                                              DECAPITATE THE
                                                          HEAD
                                            THAT REASONS
                                            AWAY THE HURT
                                            CAUSED TO YOU.

                    SILENCE

THE THOUGHTS
THAT KEEP YOU
IMPRISONED
IN A CYCLE
OF PAIN,

                                                        AMPUTATE

THE LEGS THAT
      MAKE YOU

                    RETURN TO HER.

Hot Mess
January 6, 2014 10:14am

Hot mess
you cooked up
never bother
to look up
"Hard Times"
Redefine
commitment
Just put
my heart
in tomorrow's
shipment
to nowhere.

IN CONVERSATION WITH A FRIEND
JANUARY 6, 2014 10:20AM

SHE SAID TO ME ON A STORMY WINTER NIGHT, "DON'T STOP WRITING", THE MOMENT CAUGHT MY BREATH AND A SUDDEN PANIC OVERCAME ME. DID MY VOICE DIE? I WAS MORE AFRAID OF THAT THAN ANYTHING ELSE, AFRAID THAT THE LOSS OF MY FIRST LOVE WOULD DESTROY MY CREATIVE INSPIRATION - LIKE IT DESTROYED MY HEART, APPETITE AND MIND! BUT NO, I FOUND ANOTHER VOICE AND I KNOW I WILL DISCOVER ANOTHER ME ... IN TIME, ALL IN TIME....

If I Place My Toes
January 9, 2014 4:29pm

If I place my toes
in mud would
that make it
better
speak tongues
that hover
over your crescent moons
I have bloomed
you made that so
I am now Woman.

A New Perspective
January 11, 2014 2:27am

I heard her say
inside my head,
"today was the first time
I felt separate from
the Projects,
I will never forget
from whence I came."

In the Bronx Night
January 11, 2014 11:09am

In the Bronx Night
I drive home lit,
tipsy and toppy
with my Fly Girl
blouse -
my fur collar coat
and a Newport
In between my
gold and blue nails
I AM Nuyorican
Rican
contemplating if
I should get
back with her
after the affair,
happy that I
hung out with
friends but
still thinking
of how I want
to be sweating

and breathless

with you -

or him ...

YEA I'M A NUYORICAN

Rican

typing up this poem

on my iPhone 5

High

and getting

ready to creep

up to Mami's

house,

without

waking up mi viejata

but I do anyway

Cuz' i can't

find the right key

Cuz' I'm on

Cloud "forget this Shit"

right now

YEAH I'M A NUYORICAN

Rican

For now and

Para Siempre!

If You Only Knew - But I Do!

January 11, 2014 12:55pm

It's exciting to wait
in this moist
existence
for a moment
that will be stolen,
Breast swollen
with anticipation
sweet salivation
drips from the
thought of indulging
on Earth's Ocean
platter
Slip it on and
scatter my clothes
let me pose
myself between
coffee and milk thighs
let me taste transparent
sticky honey.

Roll of the Rrrr...
January 12, 2014 2:21am

Roll the R
in deep thought
and tough times
comfort comes
From the role
of my tongue
when I sing
Celia's songs –
Alegre como
El Tamborrrr...
I do exist
in the rain
and the grass–
in the light
and the ground.
My skin is
marked with
the scars of
memory –
but not regret.
I CAN forget
all the ways you said you loved me.

Oh, Trust ...
January 16, 2014 8:34am

Oh, Trust how I cherished you
a long ago place of false comfort
that has receded into the
blankness of ignorant intellect.

Phoenix Rising
January 21, 2014 12:09pm

I've spent

I tried

I Came

you lied

open wings

broken promises

Phoenix rising.

Your dwelling in deep violet darkness,
You place no light for me to see
You stand at the edge of minute sanity
so I ask you again:
"How can I help you?"

January 28, 2014 5:22pm

My Ocean

January 28, 2014 5:25pm

My Ocean,
My Ocean,
My Ocean,
Pushes forth
and bursts
on your breasts
hydrating your
dry sorrow
don't worry
I'll return
again tomorrow
to fill the empty
space you carved
into your own heart.

On Moving Forward in a New Direction

A Hot Night in Harlem

January 29, 2014 11:15pm

It was a hot night
in Harlem,
my soul already
undergoing a
metamorphosis,
as my body played catch up
opening my
train tunnels
to the softly
roaring train
slight pain
and much pleasure
as I thought
about the courtesy
of Hindu Bodegeros:
"Thank you
Cum again!"

Three January Blankets:
010114, 011114, 01/14^2

January 31, 2014 11:45pm

I lost three separate earrings in

January

Lost on seas of ruffled

blankets

Pouring Gold rain left them

wet

My pain I released, and wept

happily

Gladly lost Two Earrings for

good

The other on hold, waiting for it's pair.

This Poem
January 31, 2014   11:50pm

This Poem
Begins with Beyonce,
Straight Cranberry juice
and my
Amnesia Search...
Will try to forget
the scarlet letter you wore
even when you swore
you, "would never do that"
it all started with a chat,
now I am here inside
my new Self
and I am beginning to
love her
and I am beginning
to let her be loved.

Letting Go, Finally

Ohh,
the ecstasy
of
Self Discovery
and the
absolute
pleasure of
putting
this
baggage
down.

February 5, 2014 5:31pm

Urban Passion Springs
February 16, 2014 4:37

If I start to write
you a poem
About how urban
Passion springs
From the most
unusual circumstances,
You'd understand
Why I indulge in
Long hidden desires,
You'd know why
The small spark
Has grown into
A wild fire,
You'd understand
That I like what we do
And why
I want to continue
This thing with you.

Welcome

February 23, 2014 12:47

Welcome to the mind
In mid-madness,
Insanity created
By bruises and
gashes.
I am no longer
Sweet candy –
I'm the taste
Of cigarettes, blunts
and Henny.
I can no longer
present the formal
Image
You loved so much
But at this stage
In my life
I really don't
Give a fuck!

ME

February 25, 2014 10:30pm

I can

only be me,

I can't see me being me

I can only know what I say

I can't know how you hear it

I can only express my emotions

I can't know whether you'll feel them too or not.

GIFTS

I BRING GIFTS
GIVEN TO ME
BY THE DIRT, WIND
AND THE WATER
I BRING GIFTS
FILLED WITH HONESTY
AND GOOD INTENTIONS
I BRING GIFTS
OF GREAT HOPE
AND ASPIRATION
FOR MY BROTHERS
AND SISTERS
I BRING GIFTS
THAT ARE OFTEN LEFT
UNOPENED
BECAUSE TRUTH
IS NOT EASY
AND LIFE IS TOUGH
BUT I GIVE THEM ANYWAY
I BRING GIFTS
THAT ALL PEOPLE POSSES
BUT NOT ALL ARE FEARLESS
TO GIVE
I LOOSE NOTHING
IN GIVING
AND GAIN THE WISDOM
AND LOVE OF THE CREATOR
WHEN I SHARE-
EVEN THIS...
IS A GIFT TO YOU!

FEBRUARY 24, 2014 5:24PM

Confessions of a Woman Awakened
February 25, 2014 4:24pm

It is here that I confess
I have closed my eyes
on nights too countless
to recollect
And imagined another's
Passion inside my being
Chest against chest
A real and warm feeling.
In our world
My breast were
Always bare
My mind always
There.
So scared,
So scared
To let go and see
What I never had
But now I'm
Here..
What was for so
Long...There.

I've Fantasized of the
Taste of Life
On my lips -
Longed for so long
For that soft
Sandpaper Kiss
Oh, for so long
What I have missed!
I am There -
Running my
fingers in patches
of musky
black cotton hair
I am There -
Under raindrops
of milk
And giving back
Waterfalls of
Honey
Mingling together
Until, as I've fantasized
He explodes
Inside every part of me.

ORGASMIC EPIPHANIES

FEBRUARY 24, 2014 9:30pm

Orgasmic epiphanies
Let me go out of my
Mind
Flip the image of
Destiny dreams
That are self made,
Growing out of
Old shoes that
Walked along
Everglades,
Hearing waves of
Pain and pleasure -
Waves that have an
Infinite Measure,
I moan quietly
Into the wind
And soak in
Orgasmic Epiphanies
Of great wisdom.

WHEN THE LAMB BECAME A WOLF, THE WHOLE WORLD WEPT.

March 4, 2014 12:45am

I Am A Woman
February 27, 2014 8:01 AM

I am a woman
I am a trio of sentiment
My body, mind and spirit
Both sing in unison and
Perform solo acts of
Expression, expectation
And emotion.
My Body
Is free and playful
Often rebelling
Against my Mind.
My Mind
knows how we met
And understands
The situation
But
My Spirit as a woman
Is always in expectation
Of unsaid things.
There are extraordinary
moments when
The Body, Mind and Spirit
Recite verses,
Collective expressions
Matching
And moments when
The Body and Mind
Conflict
It is in these

Moments that I act
On my instincts
Rather than my logic.
My Spirit often
Resolves these
Moments
Clarifying my confusion
I know how we met
And understand
The situation
It's a "thing" that
Brings relief, release
And enjoyment
It's a "thing" that
I sincerely
appreciate
It's a "thing" that
Brings me closer
To my Self
It's a "thing" that
Exists without
Complication
It's moments of
Relief, release
And enjoyment –
Moments that have
Made me
Feel like
A woman.

Poker, Pizza and Kisses
March 13, 2014 1:17am

I once shared a
White fury sheet
with a man
Who enjoyed poker,
Pizza and kisses
He often caressed my
thighs, breast
How I miss his
Scent and motion
I let him swim
In my ocean
And now he
Wants to lay
on the sand.

The Game
March 14, 2014 6:58pm

It's a game
A game between
Man and woman
Who says what first
Who can hold onto their
Real feelings the longest
Even –
Who can benefit more from
A taste of more than one flavor
It's a dance of the
War of Passion

I Water Love

March 12, 2014, 11:40 PM

I see the light when
Others see the dark,
I feel the life when
Others accept death,
I nurture the faith when
Others watch it whither -
I water love
And watch it grow.

Crack Head Love
March 13, 2014, 3:46 PM

What is Crack Head Love?

It's like:

"I let you smoke that pipe

Before me"

That's Crack Head Love

It's like:

"You can smile at ME mama

Even though you don't got

No front teeth"

It be like:

"I'll steal my mom's shit so

You don't gotta take

Your kid's Christmas gifts

What is Crack Head Love?

Like any other love

That provides self sacrifice

For the happiness of the other

So, it be like:

"Papa I'll suck a couple of dicks

So you don't gotta get dope sick

Be Like:
"Ma I'll hold up the viejita from
The corner building on SSI day
so you can get your fix"

Crack Head Love is beyond
understanding and Logic,
Defying the social norms
Of Valentine's Day, wine,
Cheese and golden rings.

It be more like:
A pig sty with bumping swines
Begging please for another
Piece of the rock
That be your story of
West Side
Crack Head Love!

To Big Joe,
Thanks for getting the juices flowing for this one Papa!

www.ingramcontent.com/pod-product-compliance
Lightning Source LLC
Chambersburg PA
CBHW042308150426
43198CB00001B/4